SEEKING HABITAT

Seeking
Habitat

POEMS BY

RICHARD K. KENT

PINYON PUBLISHING

Montrose, Colorado

Cover Art by Richard K. Kent:
Trail & Lit Leaves, Landis Woods, Lancaster, PA

Photograph of Richard K. Kent by Rogue Hazard

First Edition: August 2022

Pinyon Publishing
23847 V66 Trail, Montrose, CO 81403
www.pinyon-publishing.com

Library of Congress Control Number: 2022938238
ISBN: 978-1-936671-85-4

And so the question,
where shall we live?
And how?

Where to find
a place to rest for a while?

—from Kamo-no-Ch-ōmei, *Hōjōki*

ACKNOWLEDGMENTS

I gratefully acknowledge the editors who accepted some of these poems, sometimes in a slightly different form, for publication:

Anchor: "Just Listen"

FIELD: "Lines Written on the Day before the First Snow"

Nimrod International Journal: "Secret Passage"

Pinyon Review: "Lines for Guo Xi," "In Rural New York State, Thinking of Wang Wei," "Going Westward Within," "Fawn at the Cemetery"

The Antioch Review: "Ice Carver"

The Midwest Quarterly: "Crickets," "Dürer's *Wing of a Blue Roller, 1512*"

"Gone" originally appeared in the catalog *Approximate Knowledge: Photographs & Poems* that accompanied an exhibition at the Harrisburg Art Association (2005)

"Train," "Between Us," "Missing Fathers," "Gone," "The White Leaf," "Ice Carver," "Bluebird," "Lines Written on the Day before the First Snow," "Crickets," and "Chalice" appeared in the chapbook *Ice Carver* (Seven Kitchens Press, Summer Series, 2017)

I thank David Young, my teacher who read quite a few of these poems, for his steadfast encouragement. I also thank Kristin Rehder, who read an earlier version of the manuscript with care and candor.

— for Shu-hua

who enables many things

CONTENTS

III BIRD

IV MOON AT THE WINDOW: THINKING OF ANCIENT CHINESE POETS

V   CIRCLING LOCAL WOODS

VI   CHALICE

DECLARATION

I can't speak for others—.

But I need the possibility
of a hawk passing overhead.

I need to sit at a meadow's edge
just to watch what happens.

I need to wander in sunlit woods,
where trees have an intimacy

of their own, as they cast—so lightly—
mingled shadows onto the bark of neighbors.

I   Monocacy

MONOCACY

monocacy

The knock and glide of the name's syllables in the mouth
draw the mind back to childhood days less fettered—or so

I remember them. Even then I pondered what meaning
it had for the Lenape, who once wandered along its length:

crooked creek, I later learned. Running not far from our house,
it called me after school to its banks. Whatever slight or sorrow

may have occurred would lessen as I crossed the field and railroad
tracks to enter its domain. Its currents, though swift, I could wade.

TRAIN

~On listening to John Fahey's
The Singing Bridge of Memphis, Tennessee

The dog didn't understand
why we held so tight to her collar
as we crouched on the gravel incline.

We'd heard the whistle,
and then felt the clattering heave along the tracks,
which seemed to wobble before our eyes as the locomotive

and endless, endless freight cars rushed by with a roar.
It had been my sister's spur-of-the-moment dare.
Why *not* get nearer than fear allowed

to the train that, toy-like, passed one field
away from our house? Didn't every night
its distant clank and wail signal our entry into sleep?

Afterwards, more shaken than I'd ever admit,
I stood back up in the steamy summer air
and stared into the silent hole it had left.

BETWEEN US

The hay baler had not yet
been by. Up and down the field,

the straw, in rows, made low
golden roofs. There, in noon

sun, grasshoppers flicked away
at the cuffs of my jeans, rasped

in hot, still air, sound like
the first matches that hadn't lit.

—And then one did. And then I'd slipped
outside the stern but protective circle

to obey and obey. Yet fire, when it flares,
can awaken. My friend, our yardman, must have

seen the smoke, grabbed a shovel.
He came running to trample the fiery

swirl, while I ran to meet my mother
at the kitchen door. Memory returns me white,

shaken at what I half-understood—my face,
eyes admitting to her most of whatever

I could admit to. I suppose she knew, even
better than I, to keep it between us.

—in memory of my mother

HEDGEROW TREEHOUSE

I'd have to say it wasn't much more
than a jumble of found boards nailed crookedly
to a maple's limbs, and only as high up

as we dared to climb. It betrayed stunningly
no parental guidance. Yet, hidden in the hedgerow,
it commanded a view of fields and, beyond, the railroad tracks

that tempted our frequent acrobatics. Unfinished, precarious,
it was a platform where we performed sacraments of a kind, as we played
out that which—however less than angelic—we'd no inkling was holy.

FIELD CRYSTALS

I suppose it lasted only two, maybe three years—
my lone quest conducted in the fall, after the farmer
tilled to plant winter wheat. For weeks I'd waited.
Among ridged furrows, they'd be just glints
in the sun, sown by geologic forces I couldn't name
or fathom. But I knew I wanted to find these.
And they were there to be plucked from the soil.
I knew, after I'd gotten home and washed clean
away encrusted dirt, some of them, though small,
would be clear as a window; and, when held
to the light, they'd cast rainbows around the room.

Of open land left near our house, only that stretch
of field, up the steep hill across the creek, yielded
so many, so perfect. I'd looked and looked; and so,
in my mind's map, it became *The Crystal Field.*
And though I might have told one of my sisters,
it remained a secret place, alluring as the word
quartz, milky stone that could grow prisms—. About
any of this—no developer would have known or cared.
It might have occurred in summer, stinging nettle blocking
a way to the creek. Without warning, and as if overnight,
clustered, red-brick apartments had overtaken the field.

LINES FOR DALE

Half a century ago, what we talked
about that day behind the school at recess
I can't recall. Perhaps it was only the excited,

silly talk of boys. But your presence,
the circle of your being, in my mind remains.
Could your gentleness have arisen from a secret

knowing in your cells that your departure,
mere months away, held you already in its embrace?
I think it was March—or was it April?

We still needed to wear coats. The cold
colored the pale skin of your face. What,
in the world, were we conspiring? To remain friends

forever? Or was it just some Saturday to meet
and ride our bikes? You still wear your glasses.
You still speak in soft tones. The other kids

still swirl around us, the air still sunlit. And then
the summer somehow arrived, like this one
that now approaches as your presence returns

on this quiet, gray morning, robin and
cardinal calls braiding the world into place.
—That September the class learned of your death.

MISSING FATHERS

Saturday afternoons my father spent hours
in the basement playing cards with one pal

or another: pinochle and poker, games of shuffling
and silence, far removed from the family's din.

And though sometimes I'd venture down the stairs,
I knew to be unobtrusive as the hands were dealt.

My father, who liked to crack a joke, could
keep a poker face or also flare with anger.

What did I know of my lawyer father? What
did he know of his own, the unmentionable

one who left abruptly? Variations on
the disappearing-father act. Dead not yet

twenty years, recalcitrant oracle, my father
still declines to answer whatever I may ask.

II Ice Carver

THE WHITE LEAF

~After the painting by Bill Hutson:
Broad Street Series, No. XX

Now at the apex of the climb,
this, too, is a traveler, soon slipping free
from boundaries (some present, some supposed),
about to take its astral form, plume
of glowing frost, of ash whitening, poised
briefly now between its own becoming radiance
and anywhere—

ICE CARVER

~After a photograph by Emmet
Gowin: *Dalton Dishman, ice
carver. Dayton, OH, 1970.*

He has fashioned a boat
out of a block of hardened
water, a crystalline tug, highlight
on its bow, its whole length glassy,
gleaming even under the dim lights—
bare bulb overhead, one at the back—
inside this frost-raftered vault.

In the photograph it is 1970
and nothing is perishable.
A transparent boat cruises the dark
floor of its hospitable chamber.
Through the open doorway we look upon it.
The sculptor, middle-aged, tall, and in
shirtsleeves (perhaps it's summer out),
stands immediately behind it, his
heart at the picture's dead center;
his gaze direct but shy; lips
lightly closed, as if he momentarily
holds his breath, to let his shining ship
have this clear instant of glory.

DÜRER'S *WING OF A BLUE ROLLER*, 1512

Appearing to be mere
anatomical study, the splayed

wing fills the vellum page.
How sheared from the body

that once gave it flight …
Close to the sheet's right edge,

where how absent the bird is,
touches of ochre and scarlet

bracket tones of russet and tan.
The eye follows the wing's arc leftward—

its spread of moss-green and cerulean.
Could it be Dürer simply wanted

all to behold a rainbow's ladder
of color unfolding amid feathers?

SECRET PASSAGE

—After a photograph by Helen
Levitt: *New York, c.1940.*

If pressed, this button would ring
and ring and ring. But then what? It is,
after all, no ordinary doorbell, is it?
And so it rings at the end of an impossibly
long corridor, in a room without a door
but with one window looking out
onto a grassy, walled courtyard,
where there's never any sound
of the harsh breath of traffic,
where no wind stirs the carnival-colored
beds of roses, snapdragons,
where of course it is always twilight,
where at the center, repeating
and repeating itself, is a perfectly
clipped maze of dark green privet,
from whose heart, floating up,
one might swear there are voices.
This button—chalked on a brick
wall like a small white sun
encircled by two wobbly orbits
of planets somehow omitted
or just forgotten. Only too well
we know how it teases us,
causes that slight tingle in the tip
of the index finger, tempted as we
are to reach out, to touch it—
a child calling to us. But always
at the last instant we pull back,
wanting the letters written so clearly

and right beside it to go on and
on casting their spell, beckoning
as if to us alone:

BUTTON TO
SECRET PASSAGE
PRESS

LINES FOR ATGET AT SCEAUX

1

At Sceaux, it's 7 o'clock on a June morning in 1925.
The worn statues lining the arc of the pond's edge

stand as sentinels—some mere headless torsos—that lead
the eye into the distance. Unseeing, their presence

still pulls our gaze to them. And the folds of their stately robes
appear to echo that slight breeze in the nearby, silhouetted pines.

The whole scene is one of beckoning gods whose names
we no longer know. Perhaps you alone knew how to pray to them.

2

Yet whatever really possessed you—?
An old man who lugged an outmoded, heavy

box of a camera through empty
Parisian streets at dawn as you escaped

the city's borders for Sceaux's paths and woods,
its tangled desuetude. We know what you recorded. It's

there in the pictures that almost ache with pastness.
But what did you—and what should we—seek to find?

THE HERMIT THRUSH

~After a painting by Thomas Wilmer
Dewing, 1851-1938

The painter persuades us:

On this grassy hillside,
the bodies of two women
have fallen, although they do not know it,
into the deepening green of evening, dusk
like a lover shadowing their skin.
They are listening so hard.

Hidden in the trees that loom
along the canvas's upper portion,
painted as masses of foliage, all
the intricate labyrinth of branch
and twig concealed, the hermit thrush
calls and calls. We can almost

hear it, as we slip into the stance
and gaze of one or other of these
women, lost in their youth yet poised
to forget that too as the bird's
airy solo swirls closer (so it seems),
then dies away. They rest apart in that sound,

its dwindling. One sits with arms akimbo; the other
stands, head tilted toward the crown
of the hill. The distance between them
necessary for such an encounter
with this songster of solitariness. How
filled their bodies are with summer's passing.

NO ONE'S TEARS

Once in a great while

We see the lighted dust
We soon become, shadowed then lit
Lit then shadowed

Hearing long-prepared
Harmonics unheard before

While in the sky deaf clouds
Hear nothing

The moon hides amid halos

And as the snow deepens, the northern
Waters become still, turn to ice

Far below a fish moves

There's nothing to see but dream
Mostly misunderstood

Then—incandescence glimpsed?

Our tears—no one's

—in homage to Arvo Pärt

CAMERA OBSCURA

—After Abelardo Morell

Scudding clouds rush in to claim the floorboards.
Neighborhood houses tumble from the ceiling.

And how, on the far side of the river, did skyscrapers
like so many pick-up sticks upend themselves?

But there on the nightstand the little lamp, its shade
a trifle askew, still sits primly upright amid buildings

falling, falling! And here, large and gleaming,
the white-sheeted bed still longs for that one reckless dreamer!

III   Bird

HACKBERRY EMPEROR SEARCHING FOR A GHOST TREE

This late August afternoon how did you find
your way back to our neck of the woods? (Here

pastures and woods almost gone, though nearby
the Conestoga River still glitters in the sun.)

Your name, which conjures splendor, implies
twists of genetic code that link your kind

to the common but lofty hackberry. Our
backyard, fungus-riddled one—the last

on this parcel of farmland almost all houses—
gave up its girth years ago to chain saws. Did your

intricate wings, glowing like tiny, cathedral windows,
bring you from afar in search only of ghost limbs?

BLUEBIRD

Every meadow has its ghosts,
especially as it fails back into forest.
Towhees at the edge call and startle,
while warblers among high branches
vanish, become disembodied song hidden
amid too many leaves, leaf-shadows.
Following the ear, the eye searches,
squints until puzzling wears down
resolve or another sound distracts.

I let my gaze drift toward the clearing's
sunlit center; and there perched, as if
beckoning any beholder, a bird common
to some, to others rarest exception.
Blend of cerulean and rain-slate blue,
the robin's cousin with its rust-red breast,
orchard visitor, meadow connoisseur. After
all these years looking, I see you now at last this
Memorial Day. In the air, as you fly, blue beautiful pulse.

—for David Young and in memory of Elizabeth Hedrick (July 12,
1917-May 28, 2007)

SNAPPING TURTLE

Its shell garlanded with algae
like a green, waving hula skirt
on something armored, prehistoric,
this creature looks like it shouldn't exist
anymore. Yet here it is coming up
for air, as it noses lily pads
that partially carpet the lake. We peer
through our reflections at this
lumbering but still graceful swimmer,
at its webbed, paddling feet—
their long, almost dainty nails
like those of some old mandarin
aware of his distinct authority.

—Or is this the empress dowager
of the lake's depths? To the unschooled
eye they are so sexless–thick necks
and wedge tails–but one suspects
even these big, ancient specimens
continue to spawn more progeny.
Once out on a country road
I came upon one as large as this
that had hauled herself up from the nearby
river to find suitable ground
for laying another year's eggs—
ongoing generations mustn't be stopped.

Our boat's shadow grows longer
on the water. But the object
of our inquiry takes no notice.
He (or is it she?) even bumps
his snout on the bottom of our boat,

as if we were another half-submerged
log—*that* unimportant. As night falls,
it will swim free unimpeded, while we
grow sightless and look to the stars
for imagined comfort, for designs
half-remembered—all the glinting,
myth-haunted dots, strewn cold fires.

ON THE REPORTED SIGHTING OF A MOUNTAIN LION (OR GHOST CAT) IN SULLIVAN COUNTY, NY

I always thought you'd be back, like an eerie
autumn smoke blowing through dark woods,

watching, waiting, eyes locked on possible prey.
Blake, if he'd known about you, would have

known what to paint. He'd never seen a tiger,
but knew to rejoice and be afraid. For you, ferocious

cat, no lavish, fiery colors, and perhaps more blur
than distinct outline … His incantation still applies.

Ghost cat burning in the forest, your hunter's stare
synched exactly with just when to kill. In sunlight

you fade away; in moonlight you rule what's wild. Smoke
one can't catch, you've come back—no longer ghost.

CECROPIA MOTH

I may never see your kind again—secretive
as you are and not given to public display.
In anyone's lifetime, you may appear but once.

It was well after midnight and we'd made
the drive through dense, disorienting fog—
past Hazleton, Wilkes Barre, then beyond

past Scranton, through Matamoras and over
the Delaware, to 42 and then up the bend past
Rio's old Quarry Hill Cemetery to these woods,

summer home since childhood. And there,
with spread wings, you were right at the doorway,
unmoving in the shining porch light. Come forth

from the dark of forest shadows, this
summer night's invitation to look and look
and be astonished. And who wouldn't be?

Your patterned, regal presence: each
banded, eyed wing like its own galaxy,
conjoining at your body well-dressed

in orange fur and a white ruff; your head
topped by black, feathery antennae
attuned to all the night's finer frequencies.

When the others had climbed the stairs to sleep,
I went back out, lingering on the porch to gaze
at you again. I knew by morning you'd be gone.

BIRD

I call out to the trees,
to the air, to the bird I raised
(she'd fallen from the nest)—
a cardinal—called, unceremoniously,
Bird, a little like the one-note
she chirped in the backyard,
tangled forsythia. I watched
her grow from fledgling
to full-grown, tail feathers long
and sleek, crest fully formed.
She'd fly to me, coming
for seed, coming to my shoulder,
coming to peck the back of my neck,
letting me know it was late and
the morning dwindling. Where
had I been? Winged thing
I spoiled, cherished. My son
scolded me—having tried to make
what's wild kin. But still I wander
the yard calling *Bird, Bird.*

LOOKING FOR THE MUSKRAT
AND THE FOX

This late October morning,
the sky patched with clouds
following a night all wind and rain,
I go out to local woods
looking for the muskrat and the fox,
to catch a glimpse perhaps
of only a ripple traveling on the stream's
muddy surface, a paw print faint
in the trail's wet earth—signals
they're here at least, and that's
somehow enough. Uncaring of us,
though they are, these unconfused
confidantes for whatever burdens a heart.

THIS DRAB, LITTLE, BROWN MOTH

Now as the weather turns cold,
this drab, little, brown moth—
not even the size of a child's thumb—
has found its way to the bedroom.

I cup it in my hand, and I wait
for it to become still. Opening my palm,
I let it wander the alien land of my wrist,
fingers that become a bridge; its antennae

twitch back and forth, divining strange
intelligence. And, as I too explore, looking closer,
I discover how—no—it is not drab at all: its body
a variegated brown with a smudge

of faint gold at the wingtips, its forelegs
striped with white, its globed, black eyes
like tiny meteor specks that have plummeted
from far reaches of space. —Oh, marvelous visitor,

how can one know the fullness of your being?

WITNESSING SPRING

In the woods everything seems to know
winter's given its farewell address
and finally left. Everywhere green leafage
commands the stage, and violets—
purple, yellow, white—have scattered
blossoms for anyone who cares to look.

But at least one pair of piercing eyes
scans for something else. Perched
on a tulip tree branch beginning to leaf,
a young Cooper's hawk in sunlight
swivels its head to gaze on me. Whatever it sees—
I can't say, though it keeps me stock-still watching it

watching me. We're both here to answer
different needs, both witnessing spring:
the fierce bird, which can seize from the air
songbird or mourning dove, and a being,
caught by loss, who beholds this sometimes
splendid world alongside ever-present ghosts.

FAWN AT THE CEMETERY

We'd gone to the little cemetery amid pines
in search of names linked to familiar haunts
known since childhood, the lichened lettering
on the old graves still mostly legible.
But that summer afternoon lives
in my mind because of the fawn.

Hidden, it was lying perfectly still
behind one of the larger, upright stones.
As I stepped nearer, it burst up
from behind the slab, hastening in flight
on wobbly legs, the white spots on its tawny body
the last trace to disappear into the cloaking forest.
For one blink of a moment, that sleeping graveyard
awakened in a flash of wiry life.

IN THE WOODS AT DUSK ON HALLOWEEN

This last day of October
I watch the stars rise in the sky,
the afternoon's lavish light failing as dusk
slips into these woods I walk. Today
a new report has come out
about how fast the oceans are heating up.
Now, far more than ever, we read
the weather patterns, trying to divine what
lies in store for us—for our waywardness.
In nearby neighborhoods, it's Halloween
and some children play at being mutant
creatures, unknowing of the unbalanced
world we've made for them. Overhead,
in the pale starlight, a flock of geese passes
across the sky—the first I've seen this fall.
The air fills with their honking as they keep
together in loose formation, while I go on
along the trail, darkness cloaking my feet.
Nothing to do but to feel one's way.

—October 31, 2018

IV   Moon at the Window: Thinking of Ancient Chinese Poets

LINES WRITTEN ON THE DAY BEFORE THE FIRST SNOW

Then go on, pass through the moon gate
of the O in omen,

there where the four directions meet,
where sage and simpleton

join hands, where one walks
in the dust of fathers and mothers,

where whatever path one treads
is vanishing now with each breath.

LINES FOR GUO XI

How whole vistas so easily
spilled from your brush tip:

those mountain paths on which travelers
make their way—like the scholar, wearing

a broad-brimmed hat and riding a donkey.
Destination? It forever lies ahead, doesn't it?

Perhaps that temple, nestled higher up, or those
far-off ridges disappearing in wind-driven mist—.

IN RURAL NEW YORK STATE,
THINKING OF WANG WEI

Here, in mid-October, country roads
soon are carpeted with pine needles.

In orchards, abandoned and fading at dusk,
deer go up on hind legs for untended apples.

We wander down one road or another,
years dwindling away—haunted,

like left-behind fields and woods,
with no one now to call us home.

OVERGROWN APPLE ORCHARD SURROUNDED BY WOODS

Whoever planted this orchard died long ago, leaving
amid woods a now vague design for pursuing plenitude:

gnarled, lichened trees partially entangled,
blue- or barberry bushes enveloping their trunks.

Some seasons the old branches still put forth fruit,
though bear scat warns a forager had best clap hands

or give a shout upon entering the overgrown maze. But,
to know truly what it may yield, you must let it haunt you.

WOLF MOON AND JAY

Awakening to a wolf moon still in the sky,
I stumble out to get my wife's car running,

snow crunching underfoot. How did those old
Chinese hermits in mountain caves somehow

survive winter? The sky brightens a little. At the deck,
where I've scattered seed, a jay swoops in. On its back,

blue, window-pane feathers beautiful to the eye—like its quick,
fluted call, to the ear. In this morning's cold, it sounds no alarm.

OLD APPLE TREE

Returning to the spring lot meadow
after a hard winter, I find the lone,

old apple tree has died finally—
the trunk, with its big, ragged hole,

toppled in the grass, its scraggly
branches without a single leaf. What

now will preside over this place, its tumble-
down stone walls holding back dark woods?

LAMENT FOR NEVER HAVING GONE FISHING WITH A BELOVED POET

We could have dragged our hooks
unbaited in the lake all day. Why any

need to catch even a sunfish—
to pull the arc of its shimmering body

from cool depths we can never fully
understand? We could have left the flesh

of fish to themselves and given our own
to the incalculable mercy of summer breezes …

CODGER'S GIFT

A codger now, I suppose
I've joined that elite society

of connoisseurs of holes
in old apple trees—those

cavities that invite leaving a small gift
for a curious, like-minded passerby:

a special stone, an owl pellet, a work glove with torn seams,
a tattered snapshot of a blurred figure that might have been me—or you.

BOWING TOWARD CLEAR WATERS (VARIATION ON A LINE IN MENG HAORAN'S "LOOKING FOR DAOIST MASTER MEI")

Like you, I keep wanting to go there,
place of rippling, clear waters, to dip

a canoe paddle into depths and pull
toward the rickety bridge at the lake's end,

zone of the kingfisher that takes wing,
rattling away, and the otter, sliding from its den,

little concerned as it eyes my passage.
The bright October day companion to all.

WHAT HAPPENED CANOEING IN MOONLIGHT

In still, late-October moonlight, I paddle straight
ahead down the dogleg of the lake, the moon's twin

stirred at times as I begin a stroke to pull toward
the crooked bridge at the marshy end. But then,

startling that quiet, clamor arises—at the shoreline
a ghostly curve of wings and a ruckus of honking. Hidden,

a family of Canadian geese sounds an alarm. In muscled
flight, they lift themselves from the moon's reflection.

JUST LISTEN

Late autumn—the leaves turned and mostly fallen.
In the house amid these woods all the mirrors

now are undisturbed, the summer folk gone.
From the window, someone could watch

last light caress the meadow, the little pond
gleaming. A wind blows through dark pines,

voice saying: *For someone there's an again.*
Listen. Just listen. What once so loved remains.

GOING SO FAR AWAY

Going so far away
that near and far

become unknowing
neighbors. Who you

once were—a glint
of light, a patch

of shadow, a gust of wind,
night stars no one sees—.

MOON AT THE WINDOW

It's about time, you know. The sky reversed
and night closing in. The ghost-negative of our lives

now available for study as the moon rises,
shining just beyond the open window.

In our address books, we keep crossing out names.
Yet how astonishing to have come this far, even

though what answers we hoped to have found elude us—
as does whatever the hidden cricket promises as it sings.

NIGHT DREAMING ITSELF

Through the half-open window,
a cool mid-autumn air enters.

Far in the distance, the insomniac's
clock goes off—the late-night Amtrak train

bound for Philly and New York,
whistling again. Then, only crickets sound,

quieting as rain begins to fall, while the one
who lies awake hears the night dreaming itself.

CUCKOOS CALLING

Up and down the Sturdevant's flow
yellow-billed cuckoos keep calling—*kowlp*

kowlp kowlp, their calls to one another the sound
of wooden clogs on a stone temple floor

somewhere deep in mountains ringed
by clouds. I look into an October hazy sky,

stare into these New York woods I've walked for years—
temple, I guess—with calls of this bird so hard to spot.

ANOTHER WREN POEM

This autumn day's
blue canopy extends,

we know, all the way
to nothingness;

and, as it should be, the wren
which has no thought of this,

keeps calling and calling
in morning light.

LOOKING FOR THE MASTER OF NOTHING

~After Meng Haoran

How many times have I gone in search
of the master of nothing? His hut

is on the other side of the ridge, among
tall pines, a clear stream nearby. If I come

to call, he's always out somewhere, only
the sound of the wind high up in the trees.

I listen for a while, turn, head
for home, dusk erasing the trail.

V Circling Local Woods

AUTUMN NOTEBOOK

1 After Despair at Work

In this dusk steadily darkening,
I walk the woods without a light,

wanting refuge from the mind's ache,
wanting sheer alertness—just *that*.

Nearby, at the high school football game,
the tribal roar goes up, then drifts

into these trees that shield, while a lone
owl, hidden, keeps its counsel with the stars.

—for the many others

2 October Day along Hemlock Lake

I've come to the church of the lone pine
that stands towering in the meadow.

It overlooks the lake's edge and, beyond,
Owl Island, which on this sunlit, autumn day keeps

its station amid windswept scintillations.
A rushing sound fills the surrounding forest.

No matter how I gaze out to store up
this radiance, I cannot hold it close enough.

3 This Autumn Day

This day, for once in your life,
let the sunlit, autumn woods,

detain you for an afternoon. Put every plan
aside. Let the wind, high in the tree crowns,

blow as if right through you. Allow yourself
to fail, to become as if now no one.

This day, let your gaze inhabit the light.
This day, let the light inhabit your gaze.

4 Decades of Autumn

Decades of remembered autumn,
where woods and crows reside,

the chill at dawn and at dusk,
and at midday sumptuous warmth;

in the wind turned leaves
taking their leave; the solitary

watcher bereft but blessed,
witness to incomparable dream.

CIRCLING LOCAL WOODS

1 Path of Cloud Shadows

On this winter solstice afternoon,
anyone can walk the path of cloud shadows,

and let the ear tune in to distant crows cawing,
which might lead one deeper into woods

less known. Soon the day will end and getting
lost a little only sharpens the senses. Or it might

summon forth a whisper of a guide almost
forgotten, yet then there—as the quiet grows.

2 Heron Carcass

Over in the marsh, behind the strip mall,
a gorgeous February morning light

bathes the headless heron carcass—a fresh kill.
I've come to look at it again, the slate-gray

torn pinions, the white breast feathers
riffling in the wind. Here, I say, there is a sanctity,

though what—if any—scriptural authority
may confirm it others must decide.

3 *Galanthus nivalis* (Snowdrops)

Not far from the "Boo Bitch" graffitied
tree in these scarred, scraggly woods,

they go on with their own prayer service—
these, the first congregants of spring.

Milky, glowing in late afternoon light,
they climb the wooded slope, their tiny,

bowed white hoods in procession. Maybe
they call upon us to kneel among them.

4 Redbud Sapling in Late Afternoon Light

The shifting June light on the leaves
of this lone redbud sapling, spreading itself

amid much larger pines, becomes the only
clock you need as you stand watching the wind

lift green hearts upward, their lit undersides
forming a now radiant hem. And though so few

are without holes or edges insect-eaten,
now, in this fugitive light, they are perfect.

5 July Heat Wave

Stupefied after yet another day's heat—.
We shamble along the trail at dusk

and try to let thrushes calling
lift us out of our bodies, now letting

our eyes follow that old lure
of soul-summoning fireflies,

which every summer lead us
nowhere in particular—.

6 The Morning News

Hauling this sack
of a still dream-drugged

body on the dawn-lit path,
I've come to the woods

to get the early morning news.
What better than to cup

a stray firefly winging past
and gather its report …?

7 Forgotten Game

Who would have thought
to find a child's piled stones

arranged on a smooth stump
in these familiar woods—?

Miniature cairns marking
a momentary spell of play ...

Beneath them, still rooted,
the huge, stopped clock of tree rings.

8 Rambling in Woods in the Last Light of a November Day

All day the light,
which wants nothing from you,

had called out: The day is short. Hurry,
come walk now. Let the abundant,

crisp, dried leaves thick on the trail
rustle underfoot, their sound steadying

reminder of what matters
and yours briefly to keep.

9 The Whisper Trail in Woods

The whisper trail is the one
you can easily miss—especially

in autumn when fallen leaves
fill its thread. But if you happen

to go onto it some sunlit
November day, perhaps a slight

breeze stirring, you just might
recall things once thought lost.

10 One More Winter Dusk

As I look out from the crest
of the hill this winter dusk, just beyond

the silhouetted tree line, agitated
crows whirl past. Cawing, they gather—

worrying some big owl perhaps.
Then, too many to count, they scatter

across the pink and gray,
harlequin-costumed sky.

11 Message on this Day of the Solstice

Every day in the woods the message
is the same. It's the way light moves

through the trees, the understory, touching
as it passes fallen branches and leaves.

No beholder can take it all in. The light
goes on and on as it passes along on its way—

no matter what we may do or say or think.
What to do, then, but seek to attend it …

12 Local Woods

You can go to the woods and blab
to yourself to your heart's content,

and the trees won't take offense.
You can go and ask the oracle-stump

any question, though you'll get
no answer probably. At least

there are no locks; and, when you leave,
not even a bramble gate to close.

VI Chalice

ICE FISHING AT BEAVER DAM

We went only once. What I know
is that it was colder than I can remember;
and the wind across the big lake's

frozen expanse, under graying skies,
kept us dancing clumsily in place—feet
numbing faster than pocketed hands.

Hours passed; and, as dusk encircled us,
we realized the slick road through the woods
soon would be undrivable. And so, empty-

handed, we pulled ourselves away, the car
fishtailing as it spun from one side to another.
We wondered if we'd make it out at all.

Whatever possessed us—such novices? Was it just
that single keyhole, through the chopped ice, luring
the eye to depths of fish-haunted, black water?

PROSPER DAVIS ROAD

It's not much of a road, though it has,
unlike some here, a beginning and an end.
Its short stretch winds through woods
logged long ago; and, now so rutted,
it could easily cause a car to break down.
Some say, without a truck, you'd best
walk it—all the better for spotting hawks,
which glide away at any intrusion.

It's named for someone who didn't prosper at all,
but left behind a cellar-hole soon to disappear
and who piled, glacier-driven rocks to make
loosely defined walls that now keep little out.
Still, it's a road for maybe untangling a snarl
or reminding yourself forgetting can be a gain.

HIDDEN, LITTLE CEMETERY WITH
THE WROUGHT-IRON FENCE

No one can go there anymore—
or at least find it hidden.

I always had to look extra hard—
to spot the entrance off the highway

to the dirt road leading back through underbrush,
which in summer could be tangled and thick.

No one else would ever be around,
and soon the sound of cars

would fall away into the distance—
maybe it was the hush of becoming forgotten.

Opening the gate, I could enter
and bring the old questions—

posed again to this assembly of long dead,
and not even kin. One big walnut tree

presided, spreading its branches to offer shade
and a gathering place for sparrows and resident jays.

But then the spell would break. And nothing there
much cared about whatever obligations led me away.

Now the cemetery—"preserved," it's said—rests
in the shadow of a huge shopping complex. A nondescript,

service door abuts the fence; and bored employees, ducking
out, can grab a smoke or, stealing time, check phones.

SEARCHING FOR THE FOX DEN

On any bright October morning,
you can walk the woods along *Reynard's Lair*
and then continue north on *Far Away*
to search for that mythical fox den
the old duffer claimed, now decades ago,
was hidden somewhere among rocks, though no one's
ever found it. But finding was never really
the point. The trails may confide something else—
a last crane fly landing on a scarlet maple leaf
or the smudge of a black bear vanishing
amid hemlock shadows or ferns turned russet.

CRICKETS

A little like trying to pick out
tunes on a stringless banjo. Practically
that pointless, this sitting surrounded
by a mid-October dusk, the window
open, one dim, hallway light left on,
trying to let the call of crickets
become the mind's single chorus,
listening hard to let the whole body
become only hearing, listening and
listening so fully the mind *is*
only meadow—no matter the street's
muffled car sounds. An autumn meadow
with its long, dry grass, hedgerows,
the loosening stone walls of a farm
lapsed and passing back into wildness.
Motionless, the listener, head
and shoulders erect for the oncoming
night, its coldness, the shawl of cricket-
song lightly stitched but falling, falling.

CHALICE

Nightfall—the sky's last
bit of color cloaked, hidden.
On the street, the intermittent
hoarse rush of traffic; another
ambulance, wailing, coming closer.
Faraway starquakes I cannot hear.

Sitting.

Just sitting

to recall the self—
and then forget it,
its folly, wondrous folly,
the body drinking from the fragile
chalice of the breath
rising, falling,

unpossessable as *chalice,*
as *breath.*

Nimble mimicry.
An empty stage
where the mind,
miming, drinks.

GONE

Gone
who knows where?
Gone home. Gone fishing. Gone to the dogs.
Gone bonkers. Gone to heaven. Gone to lunch. Gone.
Gone over the hill. Gone like the wind.
Gone to seed. Gone like a turkey
through the corn. Gone. Gone to the devil,
maybe. In a blink of an eye, gone. Gone
undercover. Gone south. Gone north.
Gone over the border. Gone to dust.
Gone like driven snow. Gone. *Gate, gate …*
Gone over. Gone crazy. Gone off. Gone out,
somewhere. Gone for a look. Gone home. Gone.
Gone and got killed. Gone to God.
Gone. Come and gone. Gone, gone and lost it all.
Gone downriver. Gone upstream.
Gone over the falls. *Gate, gate,*
paragate … Like the mantra says? Gone.
Gone soft. Gone in the head. Gone for to carry me
home. Gone like smoke, like sorrow. Going.
Gate, gate, paragate, parasamgate …
Gone and no more to see, ever. Going.
Or gone, gone to see at last. Going. Gone to sea,
shining sea. Gone across the waters. How it is,
how it will be.
Gone

GOING WESTWARD WITHIN

The doorway this morning is what
happened once on a mountaintop
in Colorado at dawn, the light
signaling every peak along the horizon
to awaken itself in the eyes of all there
on that windy, reddening ledge of rock.

But it was for us to take from the occasion
a DNA-like code of glory and hold fast
to it, so that on some unknown day
we might go westward again to climb
that mountain, to thread our way
up the steepness to dawn-lit summits.

PERHAPS

The thought *perhaps*—
it can be like the flicker

of a trout slipping
through rivulets

of a stream—a promise
present but not easy

to catch, and sometimes
best uncaught.

I AM THE CREEK

Don't wake just yet … I am the creek
that flows sometimes through your dreams,
rushing with snow-melt in the spring,

or sluggish and almost still on a hot midsummer
afternoon, barriers of stinging nettle lining my banks.
In fall, I am the carrier of an endless carnival of leaves

that spin down past pools and riffles. On winter
nights, when snow hangs in the air, I remain as if asleep,
my brittle panes of ice tempting the one who walks to cross.

NOTES

The epigraph's passage from Kamo-no-Chōmei's *Hōjōki* (Record of the Ten-Foot-Square Hut) is taken from the translation of this text, written in 1212, by Yasuhiko Moriguchi and David Jenkins, *Hojoki: Visions of a Torn World* (Stone Bridge Press, 1996). Kamo-no-Chōmei's account of his austere life during a time of political upheaval and natural disasters had its roots in a tradition going back to late Tang dynasty China.

p. 42

Guo Xi 郭熙 (after 1000, ca. 1090), whose greatest extant painting is *Early Spring* 早春圖 in the National Palace Museum in Taipei, was a celebrated court painter during the Northern Song dynasty. There are many works attributed to or after Guo Xi, but there may be only two genuine paintings that survive.

p. 49 & 57

Meng Haoran 孟浩然 (689-740) belonged to the generation prior to Wang Wei 王維 (701?-759) and Li Bai 李白 (701-762) but is considered to be one of the important Tang poets when the dynasty was at its height. His biography is fragmentary probably because Meng was unsuccessful at passing the examination necessary to gain a position as an official. However, he did make trips to the capital of Chang-an, where he met and won the esteem of poets like Wang Wei and Li Bai. A poet primarily identified with the waterways of Xiangyang 襄陽, his home region to the south of the capital in present-day Hubei province, Meng seems to have written poems spontaneously in response to the experiences of his wandering.

p. 64

The second line, which gave rise to the poem's title, was inspired by and alludes to a phrase in the final couplet of a seven-syllable quatrain "Melting the Seal" 銷印 by the Southern Song Chan master Xutang Zhiyu 虛堂智愚 (1185-1269): "A pair of eyes,/black as night,/Half follow the cloud shadows/ that hang in the cold hall." (一對眼睛烏律律. 伴隨雲影掛寒堂.) The translation is by Charles Egan and appears in his anthology of Chinese Chan (Zen) poems *Clouds Thick, Whereabouts Unknown* (New York: Columbia University Press, 2010), 138. In the notes about this poem, Egan comments that "cloud shadows" is an image much associated with "emptiness" and "insubstantiality."

p. 79

The mantra, only part of which is quoted in "Gone," appears toward the end of the *Heart Sūtra*, one of the most recited Mahāyāna Buddhist texts and which addresses the issue of *śūnyatā* or emptiness. The language of the mantra has elicited much commentary. Some say it cannot be translated, but Edward Conze provides this version: "Gone [*gate*], gone, gone beyond [*pāragate*], gone altogether beyond [*pārasaṃgate*], O what an awakening [*bodhi* (not quoted in the poem)], all-hail [*svāhā* (not quoted)]!" Conze glosses *svāhā* as "an ecstatic shout of joy, expressive of complete release …" See his *Buddhist Wisdom Books: The Diamond Sutra and the Heart Sutra* (London: George Allen & Unwin, rpt. 1980), 101-106. When the sūtra was translated from Sanskrit into Chinese or Tibetan or Japanese, the mantra was never translated but its sounds were transliterated; in English, the Sanskrit words are often left untranslated. In the poem, the phrases from the mantra are without diacritics.